FRAME INSIDE A FRAME

PRAISE FOR *FRAME INSIDE A FRAME*

Whether dealing with climate change, an unsettling encounter with a bat trapped indoors, or the larger questions of what it means to inhabit a body, Daniel Lassell's second full-length collection, *Frame Inside a Frame,* refuses to succumb to the temptation of pat answers or easy binaries. Using the concept of picture frames, the poet explores his subjects from multiple perspectives, aiming for an understanding that leads, not to Utopia, "but a room next to it." Lassell is a poet of generous intellect who employs an admirable economy of words to explore a world where grief is "more / commonplace than joy," and we are caught "between question and haunt."

—**FRANK PAINO**, author of *Dark Octaves* and *Obscura*

Daniel Lassell's *Frame Inside a Frame* is a book about looking from various vantage points and perspectives across distance and time. In Lassell's gentle and capable hands, an aperture closes and opens like the valves of an alive and beating heart. I am grateful for all that courses through this collection: the wild and farm animals, the micro-moments of satisfaction and pleasure, and the indelible landscapes of Lassell's singular, poetic life.

—**AMA CODJOE**, author of *Bluest Nude*

What delights this gallery of poetic frames offers, leading us through the labyrinths of time and memory! Reading these poems is like following some Kentucky Dante through the hinterlands and, ultimately, down into the underworld to eavesdrop on the murmuring there. But what elevates this collection into the quietly sublime is the poetic voice of Daniel Lassell—direct, honest, revelatory—a humble witness to the beauty and the carnage of our times. I hope readers enjoy this fine collection as much as I have.

—**DAVID SHUMATE**, author of *Kimonos in the Closet* and *The Floating Bridge*

Daniel Lassell's electrifying second collection sits us in the middle of nature and asks us to imagine how fragile life and its creation can be. No matter how hard we try to protect our children or ourselves, it "Doesn't matter. In the end, the hardened object is a fragile object—like the body, the earth." Lassell works to build formal frames within these poems, borders not only to protect his loves but to understand them and himself. We are guided through snapshots of childhood and divinity, mercy and marriage, of a "small dog // yapping / yapping // into hoisted sky" and how we take for granted what can be so easily taken from us.

—**JASON B. CRAWFORD**, author of *YEET!* and *Year of the Unicorn Kidz*

Frame Inside a Frame is a kaleidoscopic chorus of devoted wonder. Through poems that brilliantly intensify the relentless echo and honesty of multiple perspectives, Daniel Lassell draws a faithful attention to the fragility and the fierceness of what connects us, to the forces that might leaven or level our capacity for feeling found. Bless this book.

—**GEFFREY DAVIS**, author of *One Wild Word Away* and *Night Angler*

Remarkably intimate and complex, *Frame Inside a Frame* is a gift to read—and reread. Traversing the landscape of these poems, I find myself intellectually and emotionally moved, returning again and again to their sites of transformation, their intricate interrogations of what it means to be. Each poem is "like a resurrected body" on the page, another "doorway in those woods" that opens to deepen our understanding of the world, and our complicated place in it. Lassell has written a multifaceted gem of a book.

—**SARA ELIZA JOHNSON**, author of *Vapor* and *Bone Map*

Daniel Lassell is a master of subtraction, of what he calls a *loosening joy*. The poems here are filled with song, prayer, and silence. Restless and reflective, they shift and rub against the natural world, its vastness and its granularity, with striking precision and clarity. Here, a world accumulates even as it is undone—wreckage and reverence inexorably intertwined.

—**RICHARD SIKEN**, author of *I Do Know Some Things*, *War of the Foxes*, and *Crush*

FRAME INSIDE A FRAME

POEMS

DANIEL LASSELL

TRP: THE UNIVERSITY PRESS OF SHSU
HUNTSVILLE, TEXAS 77340

Library of Congress Cataloging-in-Publication Data

Names: Lassell, Daniel, author.
Title: Frame inside a frame : poems / Daniel Lassell.
Other titles: Frame inside a frame (Compilation)
Description: First edition. | Huntsville, Texas : TRP: The University Press of SHSU, [2025].
Identifiers: LCCN 2025005192 (print) | LCCN 2025005193 (ebook) | ISBN 9781680034288 (trade paperback) | ISBN 9781680034295 (ebook)
Subjects: LCSH: Memory—Poetry. | LCGFT: Poetry.
Classification: LCC PS3612.A8666 F73 2025 (print) | LCC PS3612.A8666 (ebook) | DDC 811/.6—dc23/eng/20250331
LC record available at https://lccn.loc.gov/2025005192
LC ebook record available at https://lccn.loc.gov/2025005193

FIRST EDITION

Author photo by Austin Lassell
Cover art and design by Erin Kirk
Interior design by Maureen Forys, Happenstance Type-O-Rama

Printed and bound in the United States of America
First Edition Copyright: 2025

TRP: The University Press of SHSU
Huntsville, Texas 77341
texasreviewpress.org

CONTENTS

\\
Frame [In the underworld] — 1
The Glassmaker's Bench — 3
Mirror — 4
Seven Frames — 5
Llama — 8
Ordinary Emergencies — 10
Clay — 12
Frame [Say hello to the scab] — 13
Frame Inside a Frame [Like a resurrected body]— 14
Museum of Exits — 16
All It Takes — 17
Frame [beyond these hills a river] — 18
Temple of Salt[a smoking furnace] — 20
Ritter Park Cabin — 21
Frame [The teapot's base sizzles] — 22
Frame Inside a Frame [In the underworld] — 23

\\
Downward Rooms — 27
Churchgoing — 28
Frame Inside a Frame [The neighbor says she's been] — 29
Winston — 30
How to Skip a Stone — 31
Abandoned Farm Machinery — 32
Temple of Salt [finding god began] — 33
Frame Inside a Frame [In Eagle Creek Park] — 34
Frame [Am I lifted from the wreckage] — 35
Edge Markers — 36
Frame [In Eagle Creek Park] — 37
Blueberry Muffin — 39
Frame [Like a resurrected body] — 40
Frame Inside a Frame [beyond these hills a river] — 41

Temple of Salt [these are the generations] — 42
Hooligan's Hour — 43
Applause — 44
Nowhere for Safety — 45

\\
Tank — 49
Frame Inside a Frame [The teapot's base sizzles] — 50
Pollen Days — 51
Theory of Relativity — 52
Seven Frames Inside a Frame — 53
Road Trip — 55
On a Foot — 56
Frame Inside a Frame [Say hello to the scab] — 58
Frame [The neighbor says she's been] — 59
Hope Tithe — 60
Proximity Continuum — 61
Temple of Salt [there is none so wise] — 62
The Interior Infinite — 63
Trodden Canvas — 64
Frame Inside a Frame [Am I lifted from the wreckage] — 65

Notes — 67
Acknowledgments — 69
About the Author — 71

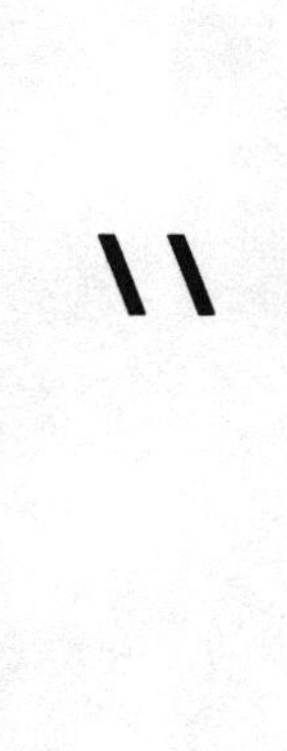

FRAME

In the underworld, I expect
no further breathing.
No air, no tension.

Why would I fear it?

Look around. Wind combs
garish pollen from fields,
the body's narrow altar

given nothing,
then given much.

In the underworld, fruition
will not matter.
Religion will whisper like
a distant pond.

On my hell-porch, I will
laugh with friends
about what the prophets knew
but did not share.

There will be no more
churchgoing, no more of that
ever-present asking,

Won't you join us?

No more holiness lobbed
as a wall against fears,
no more plotting

a fever, that if given enough
it could defeat
the advancing, limitless gray.

Prayers?

I've prayed myself free.

In the underworld, I will
be surrounded with a constant
emptying that speaks:

I am your hell,
here is your loosening joy.

The textured abyss will
cool my toes.
There will always be
another room,

ever a lowering spear
winnowing at the self,

ever a reflecting cave
or palace.

THE GLASSMAKER'S BENCH

Seated on that frame, he dims a lopsided bulb. If it asks for air, he gives it air. Touches it with water. Such devotion and tenacity, this shaping. An intention twisted into existence. Doesn't matter. In the end, the hardened object is a fragile object—like the body, the earth. Like both, a home for cruelty. Where he leans in and says, *You will be my giving or my failure*. If any mistake? Into fire. What the bench sees, and what it hopes to see.

MIRROR

I sift through dreams
and multiply
fragments.

You are
the vaporous melt, the colors
of seawater at 7pm.

You know me, you know
me.

The way you are
is a way.

I am
a recipe over stovetop,
curling in and in.

What else did I want of my body
but to make of it
perfection?

The clouds heave rain.
I look into puddles

and find in them
myself.

SEVEN FRAMES

—Kentucky, c. 2003

On my family's farm during those pensive
afternoons, our dogs searched for
anything to bark at.

One dog got a skunk to the face.

Our farmhouse, for months,
waned with an eye-watering sour

\\

off every wall, a nostril-tinge.

Those faces my siblings made
when the dogs returned,
how they craned out

\\

windows, blathering.

One night, a pickup jostled down
our quarter-mile driveway
and parked.

The man didn't exit his truck.

Just watched.

Then drove away.

\\

The next night,

he entered through our patio door, crossed
the dining room to hallway.

The dogs woke.

          This we called

          \\

                              safety.

The town nearby grew a church,
          a church's graveyard.

When the priest rose, song.
When the priest neared the altar, prayer.
Then silence.

                              The baskets passed about.

My family purchased

          \\

our home from a pig farmer.

He told us that one season, he sold all the pigs
to slaughter.
          Sold his trailer, sold his pens,

kept only his pickup—   he said he
                                could use it

          \\

no more,
asked if we wanted it.

Each winter, the rust-wept floorboard
erased
into fields.

When driving it, the brakes squealed.
The engine shook.

We perched our feet

in ghost-lit air.

LLAMA

—After "Groundhog" by Ellen Bryant Voigt

not unlike alpacas which hover
and wand through fields like metal detectors lowering chins
down to near soil some fleece of burrow and flour
llamas swim in a pasture and grass
hasn't an inkling where it's going when entering through teeth
glossy and also yellowing like corn kernels not

hovering but seated with six spikes wolf-mouth
perched as though the bone crooks silent gnawing
branches pine and neck looping upward to eye-level
angled to the head lips like a horse split at the upper end
furred and not hairy it doesn't matter how long the coat I like fuzz

which is like kissing a peach though dappled with grain
sometimes from eating so quickly with a mouth of finger-lips
to shovel back food into cheeks not kept there not in stomach
their stomachs send and receive they seldom bite open friends
I think they are mostly peaceful if threatened they will
spit like we do whap down their necks upon necks

they look like balloons in gentle wind they share fences
with chickens sheep countless flies someone once smacked
a llama's face then the llama walloped open gate-lock
bit off the man's ear and the man screamed his blood unwieldy

like a question mark the llama lifted his nose clucked
eyed females sang guttural as does a dinosaur or politician
but politicians don't hum the air don't swivel ears
with toes pinched to soil llamas seem like a poet like Berry if Berry
lived mountain-high and also shoeless bookless placeless

in America people wanting of cargo from other climates
name themselves brawny bearded fish-hooked

who would cozy to any goddamn exotic guanaco nearly tall
as the long-faced alpaca in a field both more stoic than camel
fleece cloudy like a candy's cotton maybe they are clouds it isn't
a laughable body laughter names the image don't say
because and not know why

ORDINARY EMERGENCIES

Though some call flesh a persistence
of hope, the body is a circumstance.

Some would have those lingering
at the food stamps office

beneath prayers and mildew
constructed without sound or heat.

Some would have them dissipate
like smoke from cigarettes at the entrance,

dismissed of cosmos, their personal
and ordinary emergencies.

Somewhere there is an ambulance
passing into mountains, a trio of huskies howling,

their hymns like the hurtling
of blood beneath skin.

What of those never witness to anything
beyond comfort,

never witness to the desks,
clipboards, and poorly-stacked magazines?

They would have themselves be everything.
And yet, the sun and the moon

shepherd the earth with a fishing pole's patience,
as the beautiful among us go on,

slouched without tongues,
into liquor stores and laundromats,

into the wide loneliness of gas station aisles.
Elsewhere, elsewhere.

In Estes Park, Colorado, elk pluck
flowers out of pots at the library.

CLAY

—Florida, 1991

The roofer broke his neck but lived to walk again.
The paramedics gave him a proper bed
as I pushed my toy lawnmower, plastic beads bouncing,
into a fire ant hill, where I stood with bare feet
in the forming red cloud.

FRAME

Say hello to the scab
on my neck from shaving.

I always get myself
at the Adam's apple,

as if the first man
has come up to haunt me,

kicking out a little blood,
a little hunter.

I dab the mess
to erase what I can

and rake away
the tiny spears

that pepper and puncture
everything.

I am a little less,
at the window

of a torn-down house.
I watch the cars,

their bumpers moving
battered

and in shadow.

FRAME INSIDE A FRAME

—Kentucky, c. 1996

Like a resurrected body
offered to perplexed disciples,

the shagbark hickory
shares a hundred doorways

into itself, flung open
to carve the air.

My brothers would rip
the shards free, swordfight

in our backyard, whirling,
smacking the bark

until the pieces shattered,
brittle as bird bones.

We'd peel the hickory's
fallen nuts into grenades

then lob them beyond
our swing set. Its leaves

served as roof and bed
to our fort of sticks.

Bare wherever our hands
could reach, the hickory

must have seemed, standing
among its fellow trees,

ridiculous or persecuted,
or sickly.

Did we thank it or ask it
for forgiveness?

We said nothing, felt
no stir of guilt.

Instead, the hickory
filched from us

as any tree does,
our outbreaths sifting

through its core,
a kept brood.

MUSEUM OF EXITS

Daniel Boone killed a bear
in Louisville, carved it
into a tree trunk—spelled it
bar. Now that wood
has been clipped with an ax,
placed in a museum. Power equals
preservation, which is why
the river islands, too,
have chipped away, thinned
as the glacier that carved
the Ohio Valley. In rain,
a hollowing cow's carcass,
oily and floating,
sweeps with bottles and toasters
onto a lawn.

ALL IT TAKES

—Kentucky, c. 2005

Those creek turnings ribboned upon the hills long before nearing our farmhouse, those years I traced a net of electricity strung between telephone poles, there, upon the region in the later decades yet even then, an unfamiliar memory to many neighbors. Like the horse who lived roadside, old in appearance as hewn from a coal-filled mountain, who had pulled a wagon of poles as workers pocked the hills with each row. When our car drew closer, the horse's eyes looked like dark glass bulbs, his coat peeling into summer. The day I discovered his field nosed empty all but for starlings tossing their beaks through grass, I imagined the horse, if he had untangled his knees from the barbed wire and perhaps shuffled to a river's nearby elbow. I can see him even now, standing there in my mind, belly filled and leaning toward some breathing destination.

FRAME

beyond these hills a river
slops and loops
mud gathering and bobbling
at the water's continuous
movement

where smokestacks
dropped a darkness over
this valley

and still
how that darkness
lingers
a jarred and silvery swirling
to surface

and so

how the town has hooked
this landscape

how the hills have given up
their rock
and the rock
has been in wanting ever since

how hills have never yearned for
a new landscape

the way in carving a hilltop open
with a shovel's knife-edge
the soil looks back
like a wound

and so

daylight and cattle
lumber to a ridge
their ears
flicking insects aloft

and so

what's left on earth is our
becoming

and so

what will we say?

and so

too often
a conversation softened
not into embrace

but into another subject

and so

the river's silt recalls
a slow and wordless
destruction

and so

anything in form
longs for purpose

TEMPLE OF SALT

—an erasure of Genesis 15:17-19:29

a smoking furnace
a burning lamp
bare

I was despised
in the lord

angel in the wilderness
submit
behold the lord hath affliction

I here looked after and called
his name

and lo
stricken I didst laugh
looked near and far

lord sakes
I am but ashes

behold
the lord being merciful
unto some evil

out of heaven
cities
the inhabitants of salt
destroyed

RITTER PARK CABIN

—West Virginia, 2011-2014

A bat circled my head one night.
I woke to the chittering,

sprang for a broom to hook open
the bathroom door, to thwack

it into that room, to command it
gone. When its wings

flecked against my hair, I thought
I was bitten like the laughing teens

who yanked up my mailbox
and tossed it over the dog

park's fence, or the morning
a raccoon pattered

down my chimney and hissed
along the rafters, how I left

the broom steady yet tedious
in its angle.

When I reopened my bathroom
door after the bat,

it had disappeared—so now,
it will be there forever.

That's how fear works.

FRAME

The teapot's base sizzles
on the burner before boiling,
where metal upon metal
bends the loose water away.
Congealed with light,
the vapor enters my lungs,
becomes a part of me.
I want to know the feeling:
to be water, heat-purified,
nestled into an ice cube tray,
vase, teapot. To live on after,
to have always been.

FRAME INSIDE A FRAME

In the underworld, I expect
no dinner parties.
No small talk, no posturing.

Why fear it?

Everything will be gray.
Along the riverbanks,
people will belch and fish will

bounce to surface.
It will smell like a cranky
fairgrounds.

The birds will no longer
cup solitude with their wings,
the skies filled

with inquisitive bats and demons.
Every branch will twist to ash
in their claws,

taken to wind with constant heavy
like pollen from a field,
more wandering, more fervent

than any prayer.
There will be no church-bound
stooping with ceaseless

questions about the soul.
When curtains open,
more darkness will pour in.

DOWNWARD ROOMS

I didn't know what the miners searched for,
but their eagerness made me eager too.
I wandered those uneven rooms, touched
the soot that so enamored them, the corners,
the chalk markers that pointed here, there,
that way. I was not like these men,
heaving their shoulders against darkness, a face
that doesn't face them, it crumbles away.
When they called me closer, I recognized
the rock's shape: my own. They insisted
that gems fruit under pressure, given time.
That the stories and memories of my lifetime
were asking for new light. They cheered me on
as I chipped the wall apart.
But grief is grief, I realized; it lives
enough already in the soil and forests, more
commonplace than joy. The miners enjoyed
the hunt, whereas I enjoyed the peace
intrinsic in any calm, thinking that fulfillment
rests between chaos and comfort.
The men slapped my back and laughed,
then lobbed fragments into carts.
They thought to illuminate something meant to
cherish it. *That's not gratitude,* I said,
that's just performance. But they would not
listen, shrinking into their elevator.

CHURCHGOING

In the afternoon, farmers
gather on a bench by the courthouse

trading stories of the morning:
a cow's leg recovered from coyotes,

two eggs in one roost, a stray dog
slimmed between fence slats.

A devotion that reminds the farmers
of weather, their tongues like blueberries

after a soft summer rain.
To share, to drink from that worship.

Two-by-two, city folk gather
in parks for a chess match.

FRAME INSIDE A FRAME

The neighbor says she's been
waiting days for the cable guy,

that she calls and can't
understand the pause, static.

He hangs up on me, she says.
I ask how's her health.

She laughs, a cigarette pinched
between her fingertips.

Do you see that? she gestures.
Perched on a telephone pole,

a squirrel calls down to grass
and another squirrel answers.

WINSTON

—Kentucky, 1998

He wagged his tail, waiting
for the kitchen to empty.
Then when it did, he grabbed
down the turkey.
Rosemary sprigs jittered
in the pale heat,
onions and carrots ripped
across the floor
until someone returned.
Then the whole house
discovered him.
His eyes carried up to ours:
he knew regret
by what entered and didn't
from mouths.

HOW TO SKIP A STONE

—Kentucky, 1999

Find a flat heft, then crouch and send it level, spinning across the waiting water. Let its roughest corner be the last to leave your index finger. Carry your arm through, until your waist twists. Keep your eyes where you'd like it to go—even the muddiest line, if thrown with gusto, can curve. I spent hours thumbing through the soil that summer, the same summer I woke and the bugs in my mason jar had turned crisp, legs upturned like spears. How sometimes what I'd found, I couldn't set it free.

ABANDONED FARM MACHINERY

On dithering nights, you will hear
a rattling sob coming from

those fields, calling out to their farmers,
recounting when they could not

despite all pleading and curse,
muster another year's harvest.

They've been given a farmer's worst
condemnation: a return to the soil.

TEMPLE OF SALT

—an erasure of Genesis 4:15-5:29

finding god began
in likeness

his name
all the
days lived

lived after

all the
days lived
and died

all the
days

all the
days his
name

FRAME INSIDE A FRAME

—Indiana, 2015

In Eagle Creek Park,
the soil asked of my upbringing.

It invited me into its woods,
down its trails.

To measure the world, some say
go barefoot.

But then, the rain...that mud.
The soil more measured me.

FRAME

Am I lifted from the wreckage?

No, the wreckage is in you.

Impossible to lift then, to off-shoulder
—my body, a skyward clock.

You have no wings.

The sailboats afar
steer with wind toward nightfall.

I see why they sail there: if not the sky,
the unknown of not-sky.

What else do you see?

I see a penned landscape,
an inscription of scattered reality.

You are between question and haunt.

My shadow is also yours.

EDGE MARKERS

—Kentucky, 2004

The llamas
clump against
fence wire,
staring toward
three deer
eating nearby
crabapples,
as if considering
what god
made their bodies
so similar,
so elsewhere.

FRAME

—Indiana, 2015

In Eagle Creek Park, I saw no eagles,
but instead, a Pileated Woodpecker
on the branch of an elm, that brilliant cap
of curry red and sable pickax.
Mud wrapped my shoes in clomps,
as if the earth wanted to claim me,

as if nothingness is a mercy
and absence is something sacred.
So many absences in this life.
What is an upbringing anyway?

Perhaps instinct guides our parents along
as they pass their thoughts to us,
an exchange between two hands
over a meal, all of us mashed potatoes,
cycling around, named by movement
until enough people
request no more, or some dessert.

Like the Pileated Woodpecker, I measure
the world and make it my home
—although without grace
most times not in neat, rectangular holes.
How I wish to clamp the bark hard
in my feet too, wings a covering of light,
two blankets folded over.

And a lifetime is a series of blankets, isn't it?
Each layer peeled off and layered on again,
each tragedy and elation
measured only in inches.

Sometimes blankets are altogether
missing. Sometimes I wander
without lending any thread, even to
the long-bearded man who reclines
on a bench downtown,
a dog tucked between his crossed legs.

People hand the man takeout boxes.
The dog eats first.

BLUEBERRY MUFFIN

The ink
stains my fingers,

sugar crumbling
at my touch.

FRAME

—Kentucky, c. 1996

Like a resurrected body,
a hundred doorways

in those woods flung open,
the wind with its

directional judgement,
a surety that isn't surefooted

because it spirals anywhere.
I played with my siblings,

following the sunlight's
rivulets cast along the ground,

imagination's render and us
rapt toward newness.

We sought no utopia,
but a room next to it.

FRAME INSIDE A FRAME

beyond these hills a river
purls and winnows

and so

the hills and a river
sifting through them

and so

the hills churn
a new landscape

and so

wounds
unto wounds

and so

boring to most

TEMPLE OF SALT

—an erasure of Genesis 6:9-8:2

these are the generations
perfect with god?

the earth corrupt
the earth filled with violence
corrupted of flesh
filled with flood
all food eaten

righteous

every living thing
restrained

HOOLIGAN'S HOUR

Among the midnight possums
sniffing trashcans left ajar,

find the hooligan parsing
through his day, slouched

with his daydreams,
his smile frowned

against his neighbors'
saran-wrapped lives.

He prefers a life wronged
with chaos,

the possums' rummage,
how he greets them

with his bag
freeing its plastic knot.

APPLAUSE

Because fingertips sound
of loosening bones,
                        these palms

curve away from earth,
an encounter, a wordless signal

            to describe a hunt or to praise
                        some ancient fire.

            The mind
remembers the past in the sound

of absence:

no banging,
            no clicking,
                        no vowels

just nerve endings to each other
whispers of what happened.

NOWHERE FOR SAFETY

From where lightning first
touched, where fire

burning

did speed the ground and into trees,
pushed ash into water, stomachs

burning

sickening with silt, soot,
sludge,

where animals wrestled free
of their bodies,
wilderness within and outward,

burning

spindly and brackish, teeth piercing
anything to hold onto.

Home is anywhere made hollow,

burning

and become *more than,*

a foundation leaky and unsettled,
bespoken and still

burning

as shaped as rocks to landscape,
as driven to puncture,
                    warp,
                              burden.

Instead,
          indeed—and always

                                        burning.

TANK

—Kentucky, 2002

The janitor at Catholic school lost his mother
to a brain tumor. Her final words to him:
No more medication. After a week
divorced of balance, yelling into hallways,
slamming bathroom stalls and weeping
in his storage closet, the principal sat with him
for an hour. They talked about sports, weather,
somehow about death. *Why don't you take*
a vacation. The janitor returned months later
with a new pair of jeans. He smiled at us
when we passed him, our teacher telling us,
Single file. When we returned from recess,
the fish in our classroom tank
bobbed with open eyes above the water.

FRAME INSIDE A FRAME

The teapot's base sizzles.

The water bends,

the molecules voice.

Do you hear their discontent?

The molecules thirst for ocean,
kept from it too long.

The salt body beckons them:

Come.

To you, it says:

A wish for change
doesn't concede change,

doesn't pass through you
to me.

POLLEN DAYS

the trees flaunt
their sex

you will tongue
their yellow grit

you will breathe
their sex

you will chortle
and wheeze

tinsel laced upon
tonsils

their sex
will heave into

your eyeballs
vessel-reddened

and drenched
they will

whirl their sex
upon you

you will be
their trapeze

their sex in you

THEORY OF RELATIVITY

the small dog

yapping
yapping

into backyard

then an owl

the small dog

yapping
yapping

into hoisted sky

yapping

SEVEN FRAMES INSIDE A FRAME

—Kentucky, c. 2003

On my family's farm during those pensive
months, how sunrise gifted its

reach a little farther each day,
then

\\

wandered back.

How nights contained that same
evolving,

truth without complexity
only with complex interpretation.

Next night

\\

after next night, the dogs woke.

This we called

a church,
a church's graveyard.

Our silence weaved into

baskets,

\\

then a deer stand and a phone call,
a game warden

loading a rifle
he'd named Karen.

Each season

\\

my family

erased further
into fields,

our feet

carrying air into the next.

In last night's

\\

dream,
the pigs refused slaughter,

sold and erased

\\

the farmer.

ROAD TRIP

In her 20s, Grandma drove West
without a wallet. She and her friends,
with elbows on bar counters,
thumbed out ice from drinks.
Neon signs meant meals;
they would make men like cigarettes.
At sunlight, they would chart
to other towns—those constellations
along asphalt arteries.

In her 80s, she sits by a wide cake
as Grandpa tells a story, hands in air,
how one night the moon fell
onto the roof of his car
and he cried out, *Marry me!*

ON A FOOT

I am thinking
of toenails

their purpose
on a foot

each toe receiving
one nail

their purpose
sort of christ-like

in gravity
though when I think

of toenails
on a foot

I am thinking
their purpose

as evolution without
improvement

is depressing
the world moving

imbalanced
each toe receiving

sort of christ-like
improvement

the world moving
on a foot

as evolution without
one nail

though when I think
of toenails

in gravity
their purpose

is depressing
sort of christ-like

imbalanced
I am thinking

of hands instead
their purpose

in gravity
imbalanced

though when I think
of hands instead

I am thinking
improvement

of toenails
as evolution without

the world moving
of hands instead

each toe receiving
sort of christ-like

one nail
in gravity

FRAME INSIDE A FRAME

Say hello to the scab
turned to scar

where my brother opened
my arm with a stick.

Say hello to the fir
years taller now

where he plucked that stick
then stripped its needles

to soften its weight.

FRAME

The neighbor says she's been
before.

She opens her phone,
turns a glowing image to me.

My daughter got married
in Vegas, she says.

Look at him. Met the man
just hours before,

not even a good
Hawaiian shirt.

She puts away her phone.
Congrats, I say.

She shakes her head,
I married young too.

Then she strikes up
another cigarette,

My daughter! Now married.

HOPE TITHE

a handful of leaves
offered into the mail slot
of a church's door

PROXIMITY CONTINUUM

Our existence reduced
to aperture. Pictures and their
piecemeal weather, relatives
staring without hurry
like geodes fractured into
embers. If only we weren't
so surrounded.
We're inevitable, this lifetime.
You say that growing older
doesn't mean all falling from,
but a leaning into.
If only time were that easy.
Still, how the twisting
within candlewicks converts to
generous blossom,
predictable yet
beautiful in its lowering.

TEMPLE OF SALT

—an erasure of Genesis 41:39-41:51

there is none so wise
as Art

hand upon hand
bare unto all

THE INTERIOR INFINITE

Stirred as ether,
lathered against current.

Even sand from sleeves
slips

to clumsy earth.

The angler's arrow tangles
in muddy branches.

At the banks, a clapping.

Where shadows linger,
minnows and tadpoles

learn to never trust anything
that falls

between sunlight.

Even the bugs
licking their wings

against a kerosene lantern
sound of dog nails

on a hardwood floor.

TRODDEN CANVAS

I am not a hound dog,
who can smell to perceive

a thicket's daywork mercy.
I crane from my rented porch

to sift clarity where the mower
has shaved over high grass,

blades churning and yielding
perception,

one at a time, for a time.

FRAME INSIDE A FRAME

Am I lifted from the wreckage?

I have searched
for a devotion not yoked from fear

and I notice at last

not any god
that crafts humanity.

We seek; we become,

our true outliving.

NOTES

The “Temple of Salt” poems are erasures from the Book of Genesis, using the King James Version of the Bible as the source text. No words were changed in their spelling or ordering. Only capitalization, punctuation and italics have been changed or added.

“Llama” is inspired by Ellen Bryant Voigt’s poem, “Groundhog,” which appears in *Headwaters* (New York: W.W. Norton, 2013).

Any poems based on memories or events in this collection should not be viewed as wholly accurate to the poet’s life. The art and the artist are not the same.

ACKNOWLEDGMENTS

My sincere thanks to the editors of the following publications, where these poems (sometimes in earlier versions, and sometimes under different titles) first appeared:

Arkansas International: "Churchgoing"

Birmingham Poetry Review: "Frame [beyond these hills a river]"

Columbia Journal: "Museum of Exits"

Colorado Review: "Llama"

Court Green: "Frame [Say hello to the scab]"

Cortland Review: "Frame Inside a Frame [In the underworld]"

Crab Orchard Review: "Ordinary Emergencies"

Diode: "All It Takes," "Hope Tithe," "How to Skip a Stone,"

"Nowhere for Safety"

DMQ Review: "Road Trip"

Frontier Poetry: "Frame [In Eagle Creek Park]"

James Dickey Review: "Applause"

Modern Poetry Review: "Mirror"

Ocean State Review: "Temple of Salt [these are the generations],"

"Temple of Salt [there is none so wise]"

Pembroke Magazine: "Clay"

Poet Lore: "Temple of Salt [a smoking furnace]"

Rust & Moth: "Frame [The teapot's base sizzles]," "Tank"

Santa Clara Review: "Edge Markers"

Terrain.org: "Downward Rooms," "Frame [In the underworld],"

"Ritter Park Cabin," "Temple of Salt [finding god began]"

Third Coast: "Seven Frames"

"Applause," "Nowhere for Safety," "Ordinary Emergencies," and "Clay" appeared in *The Emptying Earth*, a limited-edition chapbook from Madhouse Press (2023).

"On a Foot" first appeared in *Ad Spot*, a limited-edition chapbook from Ethel Zine & Micro Press (2021).

"Frame Inside a Frame [Like a resurrected body]" first appeared in *A Literary Field Guide to Northern Appalachia* (University of Georgia Press, 2024), edited by Todd Davis, Noah Davis, and Dr. Carolyn Mahan.

I wish to express my immense gratitude to J. Bruce Fuller for recognizing the vision of this book, and a heartfelt thank you to Charlie Tobin and the rest of the TRP team for their careful attention and dedication in making it a reality.

Thank you to the esteemed poets who offered blurbs for this book—you are my poetry heroes, and your kind words mean the world to me.

I am forever grateful to the following people who have helped these poems grow: Darius Atefat-Peckham, Michael Baumann, Caroline Chavatel, john compton, jason b. crawford, Noah Davis, Todd Davis, Haley Fedor, Benjamin Gucciardi, Luke Johnson, Sara Lefsyk, Jill McEldowney, Joel Peckham, Rachael Peckham, Esteban Rodriguez, Anna Rollins, David Shumate, Burnside Soleil, A.E. Stringer, John Sibley Williams, and those who I've forgotten to mention here by accident.

A special nod of gratitude to Colby Cotton. Without your friendship and feedback, this collection would not exist. I am truly thankful for your support and encouragement.

Eternal thanks to my teachers, for showing me what Art can do.

Thanks to my grandparents, William and Clara Kuhl, whose love for one another taught me how to exist in the world.

To my aunts and uncles. To my cousins. To my parents and siblings. To my family. To Becca, Benjamin, Clara, and James: I love you.

And to the readers of this book: thank you for spending time with my work.

ABOUT THE AUTHOR

Daniel Lassell is the author of *Spit*, winner of the Wheelbarrow Books Poetry Prize, and two chapbooks, *Ad Spot* and *The Emptying Earth*. His poems have appeared in *Prairie Schooner*, *Arkansas International*, *Colorado Review*, *Birmingham Poetry Review*, and *Poet Lore*. Raised in Kentucky, he now lives in Bloomington, Indiana.